The Three Harriets
and Others

poems by

Glenis Redmond

foreword by

Dr. P. Gabrielle Foreman

Finishing Line Press
Georgetown, Kentucky

The Three Harriets and Others

For Celeste Sherer Farmand
For Amber Sherer
For All Our Ancestors

Copyright © 2022 by Glenis Redmond
ISBN 978-1-64662-774-5 First Edition
All rights reserved under International and Pan-American Copyright Conventions. No part of this book may be reproduced in any manner whatsoever without written permission from the publisher, except in the case of brief quotations embodied in critical articles and reviews.

ACKNOWLEDGMENTS

Some of these poems were previously published in: *Citizen Vinyl, Live Encounters American Poets and Writers, Meridians: feminism, race transnationalism,* and *The North Carolina Literary Review.*

Publisher: Leah Huete de Maines
Editor: Christen Kincaid
Cover Art: Smithsonian Institution, National Museum of American History, Behring Center, Archives Center
Author Photo: @Amber McDowell Photography
Cover Design: Elizabeth Maines McCleavy

Order online: www.finishinglinepress.com
also available on amazon.com

Author inquiries and mail orders:
Finishing Line Press
PO Box 1626
Georgetown, Kentucky 40324
USA

Table of Contents

Foreword

Mule 1

Freedom Spells 1 2

Simbi: An Afro-Carolinian Mermaid Tale 4

Freedom Spells 2 9

Spells for Zero Capture 10

Every One of My Names 11

Harriet Spells for Shift Shaping 14

Sweet Names 15

More than What My Mistress Makes 17

House: Another Kind of Field 19

Flip the Script 20

Seven Years in the Attic: Found Poem 21

Dreams Speak: My Father's Words 22

Recipe for Independence 24

Sketch 25

Believed to be the First Woman Photographed with a Typewriter 27

Harriet [4] 28

Harriet Jacobs
February 11, 1813 to March 7, 1897
Edenton, NC

        Harriet E. Wilson
        March 15, 1825 to June 28, 1900
        Milford, New Hampshire

Harriet Tubman
1820 to March 10, 1913
Dorchester, MD

        Harriet Powers
        October 29, 1837 to January 1, 191
        Clarke County, Georgia

Simbi
Water Spirit
Everywhere Water is
Eternal

        Lizelia Augusta Jenkins Moorer
        September 1868 to May 24, 1936
        Pickens, South Carolina

I would rather drudge out my life on a cotton plantation, till the grave opened to give me rest, than to live with an unprincipled master and a jealous mistress.
—Harriet Ann Jacobs

Pity and love know little severance. Feelings of pity and love often accompany one another.
—Harriet E. Wilson

I can't die but once.
—Harriet Tubman

Foreword

Harriet Jacobs, Harriet E. Wilson, and Harriet Tubman are among the remarkable early Black women writers and doers of the word. Today, Jacobs and Wilson, authors of *Incidents in the Life of a Slave Girl* (1861) and *'Our Nig': Sketches from the Life of a Free Black* (1859), are read and taught in classrooms around the world. Tubman, known as Moses in her time and ours, is heralded as the most courageous and effective Black freedom fighter of the nineteenth century. Yet, although these Harriets orbited around similar issues: slavery and freedom, resistance and religion, their lives did not overlap in ways that allowed them to lean on and learn from each other. In *The Three Harriets and Others,* they find themselves side by side as if they were friends. By bringing pieces about them together in this chapbook, Glenis Redmond creates a neighborhood made of poetry. If as historical figures they did not know each other well, as poetic figures Redmond's readers get to meet them together. In their own individual poems, the three Harriets share their secrets, strengths, and struggles. They invite others over to congregate too, to sit on the porch and swap stories in the company of women they trust. While Tubman, Wilson, and Jacobs have the most to say, it's as if Harriet Powers, whose art graces the cover of this book, listens quietly, quilting pieces of her Black Madonna in the background until she has her say. Like Redmond's lines and meter, Powers' thread and fabric resurrect Black motherhood, sanctity, and resurrectionary power. When Lizelia Augusta Jenkins Moorer drops by on a break from teaching at South Carolina's Claflin College, she reads her poems to the women gathered there—and they encourage the younger woman to keep her chin and courage up, praising her direct confrontation of sexual violence, debt peonage, and Jim Crow. When her book *Prejudice Unveiled: and Other Poems* (1907) is published, those who are still living smile at the photo of her that's included, likely the first image of a Black American woman with her typewriter. In the neighborhood readers might imagine the three Harriets inhabiting together in this chapbook, there are altars for the Kongo water spirit, Simbi. No matter her surname, the women that Redmond features know they can call on Simbi's power, that they can trouble the water and not just wade through it.

Each Harriet escaped a world that demanded her submission and silence by those who claimed her as property. They refused to have their spirits beaten down or their words knocked, like teeth, out of their mouths. Their rage and wit and will were the sharpest blades in the houses that confined them. "Harriet—meaning home ruler, tested by fire." These are women who forged themselves by their own making; through Glenis Redmond's words, the essence of their work and resistance come to life anew.

Redmond brings home the point that for women in bondage, the house is "another kind of field" where day-and-night demands blended sun-up and sun-down into noxious, non-stop, work and threats that couldn't be dressed up. "This house big," writes Redmond in the voice of Harriet Jacobs, "but the way I am held by his hands, I am a tight fist. I tiptoe and flinch around every corner." The mistress's and master's prying gaze made living—and escape—all the harder. Everywhere bondage lives, Redmond exposes the mythological divide of house and field servant for the lie it is. In Tubman's voice in "Freedom Spells 1" Redmond writes: "Dey call me to de house tho. I hate every wall. I call it cage in my mind, so you know what dat make me. Can't stand mistress' reach either. . . . She tell me when to take in air and when to let it out." In these confined spaces of close-set bruisings and beatings, readers are challenged with the fact that for so many enslaved women the supposed advantages of the "big house" were a ruse. Through Redmond, Jacobs shares "I, House Nigger—not one step up from, but another kind of down. . . . He makes me feel like the dirt he walks on. Upturned and plowed. His teeth metal rakes across my skin." These poems expose the intimacies of violence and loss and rupture that Black material ancestors were too often forced to bear.

On the pages of *The Three Harriets*, these divine daughters come to life through Redmond's words, gaining inner sight and strength and accepting the praise that comes in many forms. Redmond invites her readers to sit on their porches listening and to jump at the sun with the women who call to her in verse. Redmond's poems, like the books and activism of the women she writes about, provide a "doorway into a home on history's page where they're not hemmed in at the margins."

These historical and poetic Harriets and others challenge readers to do what they have: "ink your existence firm out of the shadows. Make history one deliberate letter at a time." The imperative is to "catch what history hurls," to "double your fists in defiance and unfurl your world into long lines."

P. Gabrielle Foreman
Founding Director, The Colored Conventions Project
ColoredConventions.org
Founding Co-Director, The Center for Black Digital Research/#DigBlk
Professor of English, African American Studies and History
Penn State University
Senior Library Fellow and Affiliate Faculty
The University of Delaware

Mule

> *De nigger woman is de mule uh de world.*
> —Zora Neale Hurston, *Their Eyes Were Watching God*

she scowls all the time cause her shoulders bow underneath all that work and worry and get nothin' in return that's why her feet are planted in stubborn stance that's why she don't move, when others around her say move sometimes all a woman's got is her push & pull against the grain and that's how she survives how she plods underneath the pack & load she carries she carves out rows with determined grit if she likes you you might get a taste of her metallic wit flashing like silver starlight every now and again if she don't like you she will give you nothin' but raised hand and back turned attitude if you're wise you'll escape the eyes that rapier glare more serrated than words if you're smart you'll know better than to get into a kicking contest with a mule you'll see that she's had it tough in this world the same world that will never love her and see that she's a jewel—will never recognize that black diamond gleam she brings to the world you'll know what she knows the world only wants her for her sweat—step and groan that's why she keeps to her own clock cause she knows she will never be fully realized or idealized not in this lifetime and she's destined to die undervalued and overworked.

Freedom Spells 1
For Harriet Tubman

Deep brown. Crooked switch of a gal. Born under a serious bright, but sickly star. Measle-pocked. Faints a lot. Me, a sight: Hair never seen a comb. When I feel my head or catch my likeness in a lake, my hair's is standing up around my head like a bushel basket. Gal mostly still baby, but no slave stay a child for long.

My mama do her best wid wat she had to make me well again: victuals and a bit of de bible she done learn. She feed me both. I growed in and out of de fever and whatever else ailing.

Owned by Massa Cook. His face scrunched like a rabid dog all de time. When I still weak, he made me wade in de water to fetch muskrats. Almost drownded. He say, "You ain't worth six pence" or yell, "Ise sell you down river." I close my eyes and shut my ears, my way of spitting on dat. Dis when I become I not she. Like dat, become like dat Oak standing in de yard firm in her roots. What hold her steady, help me hold my ground.

Dey call me to de house tho. I hate every wall. I call it cage in my mind, so you know what dat make me. Can't stand mistress reach either. Seem like her eyes be everywhere at once. Her command too. She tell me when to take in air and when to let it out. Everything at my reach, but none of it mine.

I stole a little taste a sugah once. One lump, cause I ain't never had nothin sweet on my tongue. Lashed for dat. I padded myself wid as much cloth as I could find, so when she whup me, I commence to hollering. Catterwaller, but ise do wat I gots to do. I laughs on de inside. Just something between me and my maker. Five feet even and everything de Lawd put in me. Stubborn. My giddy up don't go unless I say so or the Almighty.

Field over house any day. I knows my way around every inch of work: Hoist flour bags. Break flax. Pick cotton wid my eyes close. My weight be slight, but my muscle be strong. Wid de Almighty on my side, who stand again me? In de field. I feel strength in my arms and legs. Feel what my mama poured into me. De soil under my feets and my lungs full of clear air. I earned more dan I ever owed. I put dem coins away till dey collect. I buys not a pretty dress, but two steers. When riding, I hold de reigns and I sip air as I need.

Simbi: An Afro-Carolinian Mermaid Tale

(1)

Time before, when we were not severed
from bucolic lands rich with awe/hope
one would welcome the burnt orange skies.
Us on the green land, the land
in us. We, part of the Earth—
fierce with the bright light of kinship:
Goat, trees, rolling hills and blessed water.

(2)

We see birds fly up blue high—
track their wing path to before/now,
thrum beating with wonder of the earth.
The river kinks and wanders and meanders.
The herder corrals the beast to graze.
We come to the water to drink
and we find the spirit of life.

(3)

We know clean water is big medicine.
Water is life. Without water, we know:
First the body withers. Then; spirit dies.
Neither of these are ways to go.
What we know we will always know:
The water that fills us tells us
to follow the way of Simbi. Seek.

(4)

The white men do not believe us.
Say we're what is beneath their feet.
Yet, they wrangle us from our villages.

Their bible says they must rescue us
full of our blue black savage witchery.
They think we're evil spin wicked folktales.
It's their religion that worships golden coins.

(5)

Strike of machete. Clash. Boom of gun.
We. Run. Trampled by feet and ghosts.
With deals and a plan. Terror wins.
Loaded on big ships we've never seen.
Over the Atlantic Simbi follows her ward.
Hovers overhead and around the dark hull.
The wind is both her whisper and howl.

(6)

In many fold tongues we pray—like air.
Wisps and lashes we wail loud and louder.
Our cries, the only thing we possess.
We let our strong songs overtake us—
Sometimes we sound like a blessed choir
clashing notes sometimes meet in powerful harmony.
We know Simbi will never forsake us.

(7)

We soon fear what we should not:
Water. Men. Ships. Ocean. Love. Life. Ourselves.
Stripped from what we always have known.
Cycles. Seasons. Spirals. Drought. Gift. Simbi. Water.
Where have we failed? In trust? Dust.
Doubt. Loss. Blood. Chains. Stolen. Lost. Torn.
We'll never be what we once were.

(8)

We're now shadows of our better selves.
We are severed people. Enslaved. Not slaves.
We do not know our station yet,
chains. Shackles. Manacles. Clang. Clang and lock
at our wrists and at our ankles.
Bodies side by side we're rubbed raw.
At our open wounds they throw salt.

(9)

On weaken legs they make us dance.
This long nightmare we keep on reliving.
We remember when we danced for Simbi,
offered up our soul to please her.
On steel leashes we jerk and dangle.
Inside die in this face of evil.
When we trance dance we must remember.

(10)

The West says, Mermaid, but she's more.
Simbi sits in the pantheon of Spirits.
She dwells in oceanic blue black depths.
Water. Born. Fed. Water. Wise. Water. Wielder.
Whirl. Warrior. Wailing. Waves fierce long arms.
At each end fist: fight or hover.
Her reach is either house or jail.

(11)

Simbi there. Cymbee here. Name her. Moot.
People of the Congo know her well.

Simbi's spirit must be honored and fed
with each drink, food, dance and treasure.
Without ceasing, she finds reasons to mother.
Wraps her long arms around her people
on either side of the deep Atlantic.

(12)

Come rain. Come flood. Come torrent. Come.
World's balance is off when Simbi's caught.
Until Simbi free we don't know work.
Sit. Sleep. Rest. Pray. Eat. Think. Dream.
We got plenty of sense. Know where
our beautiful blessings come from. Sea. Deep.
Knee-bent we sing for full body release.

(13)

We are blooming starsseeds captured, we rise.
We are black water bodies southern beached.
Snatched and tied to land by hands.
We told, but full of telling. Story-filled.
Beware of the lowly ones who overcome.
The one that hits soon forgets. The
one that takes the hit never forgets.

(14)

Know there are two kinds of people.
Those who have Simbi. Those who don't.
We have Simbi. Ocean-filled vessels seeking more.
We are the song of the sea.
We are that which can't be named.
We are blue, green, gray, black cosmos.
We leap on dry land. Find water.

(15)

In our tears, sweat and stolen kisses.
We keep our history wet in memory.
Every act we make. River and pond:
places of true hallow ground for Simbi.
We find ways to worship and swim.
We, the blackest blue beauty. Carolina bred.
Ancient lights. Stolen, but belong to Africa.

Freedom Spells 2
For Harriet Tubman

Words full of heat. Dat where power be, if de come from de right place. So, I set mouth to pray. Speaks wid my whole self to pry Massa Brodess heart open. Wid dis tool. I speak in Jesus' name. I do my best to wrench de devil's hold. I prays wid out ceasing from sun up to moon out. I hold fast. I mumbles. Sometimes I shout in de field. If my heart takes to sing I sings. Come by heah lawd. Come by heah. See if dis song be a key to open de gate. Release dis five finger grip, Lawd. We bound by dey law. Though it crooked as a creek. We's worth more dan de money we put in his pocket, but greed speak louder dan truth to him. Greed be winter. Be cold wrong. Holding us against our time. We done wet dese field wid both sweat and tears. Skutch flax. Toted de lumber. Our feet done walk every step of dis ground. When prayer don't turn massa's mind. I turn. Change prayer to curse: "Lawd, if you ain't never going to change his heart, Kill him." He died soon after. I say de word be power. Gotta mind which way you use it. Cut two ways. I wept on it a lil, but dat was just a passin fog. Cause I fix my mind on how he kept mama 10 years longer as a slave. I study on dat. Wipe my mind clear. I fix myself. Take marchin' orders from de almighty. He speaks. I rise up. He ain't got to tell me but once: flee.

Spells for Zero Captures
For Harriet Tubman

Conduct like I ain't tryin to die. Leave when de moon new. Sky dark. Listen to what's on my inside, 'cause it don't lie. When my chest flutters, I knows danger lurks. Change course. "Know I can't die but once." But, ain't tryin to do dat just yet. Don't speak on nothin. Proud talk get you dead. No need for I did dis. I did dat. No peacocking. Blend into tree trunk. Travel during winter. Buy time. Saturday night rewards for runaways not in papers till Monday morning. Got a whole day before dey 'spect we gone. Read people and de land like white people read books. When I have a spell, shout not. Don't fight deep sleep. Go into de body quake. Vision and dreams be how God directs my path. Follow de map dat my inside knows. Let God talk. No open field in daylight. Know de codes like I know de woods. Light in window. No trails. Cover footsteps. Don't give into thoughts of coon dogs and guns. Quiet steps. Silence. Give babies de root. Paregoric. My Grandma Modesty came over on de boat from Africa. She knew the earth holds medicine. Don't tarry. Make friends of weary and tired. Dey don't leave nohow. "You'll be free or die." Listen to de old ways. Don't turn back. Trust de Quakers, but carry gun loaded. Curse slavers. "Never wound a snake; kill it." "God's time Emancipation is always near." He set de North Star in de heavens. He gave me de strength in my limbs to follow where his light leads.

Every One of My Names
For Harriet Tubman

Every one of my names I earned.
cept de first: Araminta Ross.
Given to me at birth.
Didn't take too much to it.
'cause sounds like a flower standing in a field.
Araminta. Araminta. Got God's covering.
I keep de prayer and music from it.
For short dey say Minty.
I like how dat sing.
Got more of my sting.
I stood up to massa no matter
who was wronged,
massa head-butted me
into dreams and visions.

Took Tubman from my man.
My husband left me,
cause I wouldn't stay put.
He wanted me rooted
to his need and de cabin.
One of de times I was gone
I came back, he in de arms
of another woman.
He axed me in de middle
of my heart with dat.
Lawd knows I loved him,
Lawd knows he loved me too,
but I was meant for more.
I belong to de many.

Dey calls me Harriet.
I took Harriet from my mama.
Her love circle around me
like my wrap around my head,

like my shawl hugs my shoulders.
Dey call me brave, cause I wrap
my long arms around my peoples.

Dis how I stand: rooted and ready for battle.
Dis is how I love—fitted for fight.
My face is not fixed on pleasing—
what good is a smile in war?
I busy in battle.

Called me Conductor too
cause I head dis foot train
with hounds at my bloody feet.
I still runs.
I runs and I runs.
I told Fredrick Douglass once
I ain't never lost a passenger.
I know which way is North
with my ear to God's mouth.

General too dey call me,
cause I at de head,
where no woman supposed to be,
but I outsmart every slaver's hunt.
Fear for what?
Once I break chains, I release
de minds on being a slave next.
No matter what dey call me—
I'm on a mission.
If dey even thinkin about turnin back,
I point pistol to head.
Say, a dead negro tells no tale.
Dis de way my spirit rise up.
My fire be both a curse and a blessin.
Dis fire burns—never snuffed out.

Dey call me Moses—
mah people mus go free.
Dey whisper me spy too,
when dey speak of me
cause I got my hand
in so many plots.

Dey give me names most of dem mannish—
but by God's grace I go
wid a long skirt
with these able hands
to answer every call.
—all woman.

Harriet Spells for Shift Shaping

Being looked over, around and through my best weapon. Turn into whatever de time of day call for. Pitch black step. Slip into owl or hawk. Turn tree trunk. Become de hound chasing you. Lead de pack to river edge. Invisible. Brown bird always best. Mourning Dove, crow, sparrow, railes, crakes and coots. Like old black woman. Dey not spectin nothin' but an old slave. Look closer. Common brown bird. Last time I checked brown birds got wings too.

Sweet Names
> *A spirit that was craving healing mercies*
> —Harriet E. Wilson

I crave, puddin, pumpkin and sweet potato.
Sweet names my papa calls me,
Sweet names my mama calls me
but only in my dreams.
There her soft orange song wraps
around me like a warm quilt I never had.
In my dreams her words and arms
swaddle me far from hunger's mouth,
far from its sharp white teeth
that tear through me like Winter.
I was born with the spoon of lack
on my tongue. It leaves a bitter taste.
So, I always long to hear my mama's voice;
not raised in anger, but low
with the sweet whisper of baby
spoken with a kindness
that washes away worry.
This is just a dream,
but dreams are all I have
not shackled or chained.
So, I hold onto them,
but they are made of clouds
like my mama's love
that I cannot touch.
My dark skin stills her like stone
when she looks at my face
a wall grows high and wide.
The blood meant to bind,
does not circulate between us.
The blood that runs in my veins
is tainted by her so called sin.
This belief is pinned
to my mama's heart
by her own hand.

I am her cameo of shame
pinned to her for life.
My silhouette outlines the darkness
she fell into. Low is her station
in the eyes of others—in her own Irish eyes.
I am the blight she bore with a black man
She cannot see the good in me.
Comely I might be, but I will never know
Her eyes are the only mirrors I possess.
Regret is the reflection she sheds.
I could be a good fruit,
but I am treated as a rotten seed,
a load my mama could no longer bear.
She gave me away.
If she ever called me sweet names,
puddin, pumpkin and sweet potato
those kisses did not linger.
All I have is ache,
so I fill myself with dreams—
eyes not closed in sleep,
but wide open with want.

More than What My Mistress Makes

> *There seemed no one capable of enduring*
> *the oppression of the house but her.*
> *—Harriet E. Wilson*

Born free I was still dragged
by my spirit from sun-up to sundown,
a daughter of a hooper of barrels,
a daughter of a washerwoman.

My knuckle's blood, my mama's
callused legacy. My curved spine,
my papa's inheritance. My dark skin;
hung on me like a shadow. With it

I face the heat of hate. I lived my childhood
dome squashed singed by my mistress' breath
housebound pressed, lash-tied to obedience.
Dragged by my spirit from sunup to sundown.

My neck squirms to somebody else's clock.
I swing to this borrowed cadence.
My dance is drag, shuffle and kick ball chain.
I dangle to the strain of a short leash,

a tightened noose, with a tag, Our Nig.
This is how I am called
less than the family dog.
Under my tongue there is prayer.
Under my tongue there is civility,

but no one would ever know,
because my mouth is tamed,
my dreams squelched, but I am more
than what my mistress makes of me.

I am fashioned by a force greater
than her will, stronger than her rawhide slash,
boot tip and poison whipping of words.
My mistress always makes a cruel point,

but my rage is the sharpest blade
in this house, a keen tip fashioned
by her edge. I am destined to slice strife.
In my chest a hurricane stirs my heart,

the woosh sounds like a familiar friend.
Harriet my name, an elixir I drink
when pressed between earth and sky.
From this deep well I find the more.

More than what my mistress makes of me.
In my heart I am stirred—not by Our Nig,
but my true moniker, Harriet—
meaning home ruler, tested by fire
I forge myself by my own making.

House: Another Kind of Field
For Harriet Jacobs

This house big, but the way I am held by his hands, I am a tight fist. I tiptoe and flinch around every corner. Over my shoulder is where my eyes live. This body I carry, not mine. My chest heaves all day. High yellow. Light Bright. Almost White. Whatever color I am called—his gaze burns me, so does his hands. I am kept closer than his wife. He leaves me nothing, but bruised blue. I, House Nigger—not one step up from, but another kind of down. House, be another way to say: field. He makes me feel like the dirt he walks on. Upturned and plowed. His teeth metal rakes across my skin. His mouth and his hands don't do nothing, but take: rip, tear and thrust. I bleed and breed. Chains seen or unseen, my feet, still shackled. This is not the life the Almighty meant for me, but no choice is what I got. The only place I run far is my mind. I keep my lips shut, but every scream I don't shout is loud within me. Every scream adds up to flee. My feet become my mind. They carry me to where Grandma stay. She free. How I'd like to just lie down in her arms and rest for always, but ain't no rest for a hunted slave. Light Bright. Almost White. Whatever color I am called—his gaze finds me. This body I carry, not my own. My chest heaves all day. Grandma attics me away. When I walk through her upstairs door, I don't know if I will ever return. This attic feels like a pine box. My feet can't wander many feet yonder, but a few steps. My hands, my arms, my legs God gifted me can't stretch. I am a bent star dwelling in shuttered light. So small my world seems. Low roof and tight walls make like my grave. This attic could be a pine box closing, but in my chest, I feel an opening. Above his reach, the less I feel like a kept thing. This room dark most days, but I see myself clear. I dance a dance in this place of tight walls and roof to break his white grasp. I wiggle. I weave. I work—not seven days, seven weeks, seven months but seven years of bearing heat and cold. Where rats bite—the only touch I know. I am bent by this stay, but I fix my mind for when that door opens. I am ready to fling myself and take up any space in this world star-wide. Fully free and human.

Flip the Script

$100 REWARD for JAMES NORCOM.

The above reward, with all reasonable charges, will be given ▆▆▆▆▆▆▆▆▆▆▆▆▆▆▆▆▆▆▆▆▆▆▆▆▆▆▆▆

All persons are hereby forewarned against harboring or entertaining ▆▆▆ or being in any way instrumental ▆▆▆ to his escape, under the most rigorous penalties of the law.

▆▆▆▆▆▆▆▆▆▆▆▆▆▆▆▆▆▆▆▆▆▆ HARRIET ▆▆ light mulatto, 21 years of age, about 5 feet 4 inches high, of a thick and corpulent habit, having on her head a thick covering of black hair that curls naturally, but which can be easily combed straight. She speaks easily and fluently, and has an agreeable carriage and address. Being a good seamstress, she has been accustomed to dress well, has a variety of very fine clothes, made in the prevailing fashion, and will probably appear, if abroad, tricked out in gay and fashionable finery. As this girl ▆▆ designs to transport herself to the North.

Seven Years in the Attic: Found Poem
For Harriet Jacobs

The Secret of The Tarot by Eugene

    "Angel number 7 an auspicious sign
    from our guardian angels

    that we are on the right life path, when
    we see angel number 7 again and again,

    it means that we will overcome all obstacles
    and realize success in our endeavors.

    Angel number 7 is a message from the angels
    that they are happy with the choices

    that you have made. Continue on
    your present path you will be rewarded."

Dreams Speak: My Father's Words
    For Harriet E. Wilson

I had to coax my heart open to see
what my bones already know. Follow

how the blood road travels back
to understand—how the tree root shoots

from solid ground. If I stand still
long enough, I can feel how the earth turns

by my father's dark hand. How he lifts
the veil, so I can stare into the worlds

between the worlds. The branched bottles
hold his clear voice as he dream speaks

in my ear. Shows me how destiny's wheel turns.
How trouble will hound me most of my days.

How grief will rob me of my son,
my beloved held at my breast. How work

will do its best to beat my body down.
He says trouble will stand next to me

like kin. Bedridden, I will beg to die.
But he chants, fair daughter, you will rise.

You will rise and follow the leaves.
The call of my dream voice will guide you

to trace your palms. Close your eyes.
Feel the pulse. See how the future connects

to your strong lifeline. Your legacy
blown on bottles, etched in books.

Gifts held by others. You will be known:
The Earnest Eloquent Clairvoyant.

On this dirt path paved, you will conjure
what the world hands you. Navigate the heart.

Your palms smooth jagged rocks into fortune.
Divine daughter dance between those worlds.

Curtains drawn open. Peer. Gain inner sight.
See how at the core all turns and turns.

Recipe for Independence
For Harriet E. Wilson

First learn my letters.
Read people like words.
Capture heartache and Joy.
Pen it to the page.

Stir and Stir.
Multiply every gift God gave me.
Use liberally
like the hair dye
I made.

Turn a sheet.
Dust a chifforobe.
Tell a fortune.

Take out an ad: Earnest Colored Clairvoyant.
Connect people from this world
to the next.

See what people need.
Sell it to them
along with their wants:
Embody and bottle dreams.

Sketch

Draw the face so we may stare
at the rotten teeth truth.

>Give yourself a pristine mouth
>to say your piece, a crude doorway

into a home on history's page
where you're not hemmed in at the margins.

>No begging or bowing.
>Stand in your place.

Ink your existence firm out of the shadows.
Make history one deliberate letter at a time,

not as slave but not fully free either.
Write it the best you can.

With a determined hand, write the wrong.
Right it! Press your free hand upon parchment.

>Spill ink like night clouds
>that clot what your soul cannot hold.

Catch what history hurls.
Double your fists in defiance,

>unfurl your world into long lines.
>Get straight to the point:

Pen every deed. Record the heavy dreams
that woke you each morning.

      Press down. The paper can bear your weight.
      Make the page speak of backbreak,

Let your quill quiver with nothing less than the meat of it.
Whip the naked flesh of the past like you were slashed.

      Bleed deep—Gash history
      even if it must stand on hobbled legs.

      Press your free hand on your heart.
      Unbind your mind no matter

how the hand wavers.
This is how perfect penmanship feels

      one liberated turn after the other.
      Head the helm. Write your ending.

Right the sky. Burn through fog, mist and muck.
Through your eyes, pen a new horizon

      pulled and drawn by your own hand.

Believed to be the First Black Woman Photographed with a Typewriter

Portray a notion they have never seen:
me, poised—proud by my prized article.
Show them I am serious about words.
My head and back not field bent—
fully proving that I pluck only letters.
Capture my black visage always beaming, so
they will remember: Lizelia Augusta Jenkins Moorer.

Born: September,1868 Pickens, South Carolina, U.S.
Died May 24, 1936 (age 67)
Orangeburg, South Carolina,
Poet, teacher and civil rights activist

Harriet [4]
> *For Harriet Power*

The fingers find other ways to write:
Pierce the needle's eye pull thread through.
Make-do be how I'm made up anyhow.
Look around. See what's at hand. Gather.
Listen deep within to what God say.
Cut cloth after the message come clear.
From lap spin tales with able hands

With Thanks

Thank you to Dr. P. Gabrielle Foreman for providing groundbreaking research, as well as inspiration through fruitful conversation about Harriet E. Wilson and the others. My poems gained a solid foundation because of her scholarship. Thank you to Lynnette Overby for being the intuitive thread in bringing the three of us together like our own modern-day version of the Three Harriets. Through Dr. Overby's invaluable talent and leadership, she made it possible for her students to dance The Three Harriets to life on stage across the world. The dancers were Amber Rance as Harriet Jacobs, April Singleton as Harriet E. Wilson, and Ikira Peace as Harriet Tubman. They each gracefully lifted my words off the page and landed them palpably onto the stage. Thank you to Ann-Thomas Moffett for dancing poignantly as the young Harriet E. Wilson's mother. Thank you to my twin daughters, Amber Sherer (Harriet Jacobs) and Celeste Sherer Farmand (Harriet E. Wilson) for the speaking Harriets in the production at the Peace Center. It was a mother's joy to be flanked creatively by my daughters. Thank you to Ralph Russell for composing powerful music for the dancing Harriets. Thank you to the Peace Center in Greenville, South Carolina to be the first site to present shows for students. Thank you to early readers of this manuscript: Jaki Shelton Green, Margaret Bauer, Amber Flora Thomas, and Tara Betts, Lynette Overby. Thank you all for your words via blurbs, your words grace this volume and offer praise allowing me to affirm my poetic trek to keep writing in the voices of the Three Harriets.

Glenis Redmond is an award-winning performance poet from South Carolina. She received her B.A. in Psychology from Erskine College. She left the counseling field in the 90's to begin a career in the literary arts. She started out traveling statewide as a teaching artist with the South Carolina Arts Commission. In 2000 she signed with an artist's book agency based in Asheville, North Carolina. She toured 10 months out of each year earning her the title, Road Warrior Poet. She has toured to almost every state in the country and traveled internationally to London, England, and Haiti. She has also traveled to Muscat, Oman for the US State Department's Speaker's Bureau and her work has been featured at the Dance and the Child International in Adelaide, Australia in 2018.

While touring Glenis earned her M.F.A in poetry from Warren Wilson College. Afterwards, she obtained two poet-in-residence posts, one with the New Jersey State Theatre in New Brunswick and the other in her hometown with the Peace Center. Glenis has been a literary community leader for almost thirty years. She is a Kennedy Center Teaching Artist and a Cave Canem alumni and has been the mentor poet for the National Student Poets Program since 2014. In the past, she has prepared these exceptional youth poets to read at the Library of Congress, the Department of Education, and for First Lady Michelle Obama at The White House.

She has three published books: *Backbone, Under the Sun*, and *What My Hand Say*. In 2022 along with the *Listening Skin*, she will have two others published: *The Three Harriets and Others* (chapbook) and *Dave the Potter: Art and Poetry for David Drake* by Jonathan Green and Glenis Redmond, University of Georgia Press in December.

She is a North Carolina Literary Fellowship recipient and helped to create the first Writer-in-Residence at the Carl Sandburg Home National Historic Site in Flat Rock, North Carolina. Her work has been showcased on NPR and PBS and has been most recently published in *Orion Magazine, The New York Times, storySouth* and the *North Carolina Literary Review*.

Glenis has been awarded the Charlie Award by the Carolinas Mountain Literary Festival. in honor of Charles Price. She also received the highest art award in the state of South Carolina, the Governor's Award in 2020. Glenis will be inducted into the South Carolina Academy of Authors in April 2022.

www.ingramcontent.com/pod-product-compliance
Lightning Source LLC
LaVergne TN
LVHW041558070426
835507LV00011B/1164